My Baby's First Islamic Words

From Letters A to Z

For Ages 2-6

BY THE SINCERE SEEKER **KIDS** COLLECTION

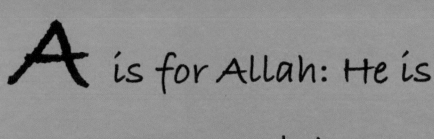

A is for Allah: He is our Creator and the One that takes care of and looks after us.

B is for Barakah: Allah loves us so much; he gifts us from small things to BIG things.

C is for

charity: we always try to help people in need.

Charity Box

D is for Dua: we ask Allah for everything with our parents, and when alone.

E is for Eid:

Muslims have two holidays to celebrate with their families and friends each year.

Eid Mubarak

F is for

Five Pillars: which every Muslim must practice in their life.

G is for Gabriel: the name of the Angel that brought down the Holy Quran to Prophet Muhammad peace be upon him.

H is for Hadith: sayings of Prophet Muhammad, peace be upon him, that teach us about Islam.

I is for Islam: the religion and way of life of a Muslim.

J is for Jannah: which Muslims will be gifted if they believe in God, worship Him, and be good.

K is for Kaaba: the House of Allah where Muslims face to pray to Allah every day.

L is for

Love: love comes from Allah. He loves us very much, and we love Him too!

M is for

Muslims who believe in and worship the One God.

N is for Nabi

Muhammad, peace be upon him: God sent him to us to teach us about Allah and Islam.

محمد

صلى الله عليه وسلم

O is for O-
Allah: we call
Allah for
everything we
need, and He
listens.

P is for peace: Islam
is a religion of peace
and love.

Q is for

Quran: Allah's final Book and Words to teach us about Him and Islam.

R is for

Ramadan: the special month when Muslims fast by not eating and drinking from sunrise to sunset.

S is for salah: we pray to Allah with our family or by ourselves five times a day.

T is for

Tawheed:
Muslims
believe in
and
worship
only One
God.

U is for Ummah: our Muslim community.

V is for Veil:

Muslim women use one to cover their hair and chest because Allah asked them to and so that they stay humble.

W is for

Wudu: Muslims use water to wash parts of their bodies before praying to God.

Y is for Yusuf, peace be upon him: one of God's Prophets who was left in a well by his brothers.

Z is for Zam-Zam Water: blessed water from the well of Zam-Zam in Mecca.

Printed in Great Britain
by Amazon